I0663878

in my universe

ida-sofia

Written, Illustrated, & Designed by Ida-Sofia
Edited by Emily Rooker

ISBN-13: 978-1518766459
ISBN-10: 1518766455

www.ida-sofia.com

this book is for those of you
lost in your own universe

emily,
thank you for
your kindness +
friendship.
you are the best ♥

leh

create your universe

the left pages in this book are intentionally left blank, allowing you to express your creativity beside my words.

write, draw, paint - do whatever you wish to create your own universe,

and find yourself within mine.

create your universe

chaos

"chaos was the origin of everything,
and the first thing that ever existed."

create your universe

i am calm
i am quiet

but the thunder
inside of me

will start fires
and destroy you

create your universe

when i run to escape,
i am chained to my thoughts

held captive by the dust
that collects in my atmosphere

they tell me, "just breathe"

that's the very thing
that will kill me

create your universe

you said, "let's take it slow"
your hands said otherwise
maybe i'm not myself
but i've tried

tell me how to
be enough
feel enough
show enough

intoxicated with emotion
drunk on misspoken words
i want to live inside the pain
i feel when you're away

"i'll miss you too,
but i'm not going to
think about it"

create your universe

i could feel you
forgetting
slipping into
the abyss

i'm still here

the flowers you
planted in me
are very much
alive

create your universe

cruelty laced with delicacy
reason wrapped in ecstasy
i never knew i needed this
until i stepped away

clouds dancing circles around
what is left of ourselves

i don't know me anymore
but why would i want to?

create your universe

we cling to similar souls for the feeling of comfort, as if anything is better than being alone. we lay to rest on one side of the bed, hoping that someday, another starving mind might just join us and make us feel warm. we cling to each other, we search for "togetherness", we decompress to the idea of sharing our thoughts. we'll mindlessly settle for someone blatantly wrong for us. as if anything is less painful than being alone.

create your universe

if time is nothing
but a string of numbers
the time spent in your arms
was indefinitely forever

and i swear
i could have
loved you.

create your universe

i watched you leave this life
though you promised to be mine

i watched your goodbye shift tides
and disrupt lives -

still i ache for the return
of my missing light

create your universe

hearts are not for
origami. you cannot
twist and fold my
heart until it is art in
your eyes.

create your universe

i stepped out into the world, afraid of the fickle
sunlight and its warmth. nothing was ever predictable
anymore. i wouldn't have been surprised had the sky
been red and the clouds black. maybe raven's would be
white, and dove's black. maybe i could be life, and you
could be death. we could walk hand in hand until the
universe tore us apart. but it wasn't the universe that
stopped me.

i held a letter in my hands,
one i had written and never let go.

it wasn't as if i had come to my senses. my emotions
had not yet gathered themselves into a pattern. they
were not a puzzle i could piece together. there were
always pieces missing, and pieces that i had not yet
even formed. the notion of change was as inconsistent
as it had always been in the past. my past had no
meaning except for the times i could remember. my
heart had still not healed.

i ended my letter with, "i've lost a lot in you," and
watched it graze the sky with blue cursive.

create your universe

you were every love song
and heartbreak i had ever known;
all at once

create your universe

but you were strong, and i was fragile
when you took my hand, you took my worries
when you pulled me close to you
my aching heart would quiver

and as i had feared and expected,
i could not be the one to take the pain away.
i could not be the hero, the savior, the medicine.
i could not be your cure.

but you were mine.

create your universe

i am a ghost
that follows you
in high spirits

longing for
what once was
the light of my life

create your universe

what is it about you? what is it about your affection
that leaves me longing for more? you keep me on
my toes. you keep me thinking about you. but you
are not the one.

i cannot go on with this pit in my stomach. the
longing becomes too deep. the cuts are too fluid.
nostalgia takes me like a wave in the pacific. i do
not know how we got here, and it's not here that
i want to stay. you can be the songs i write, but i'd
rather have you be the one to sing me to sleep.

create your universe

the stillness was silencing -
an all encompassing fear
the most pure blend
of mystery and kindness

how can i drown
in an ocean of love,
if the waters do not
pull me under?

create your universe

sometimes i feel you
pull me out of the
darkness

and sometimes,
you place me there

create your universe

if thoughts were like fire
we could burn what is
left of our fears

we could set off explosions
in our eyes, become blind
to the chaos erupting
around us

just one look
could turn me to flames
a monumental destruction

maybe you'd
extinguish
me

create your universe

if i could write about longing
and the pain that dwells
inside of me in your absence

i would let the world know
of your wonder and compassion

and how hollow i am without you

create your universe

you have caused
the most lavish
fever in me

an undoubtedly pure
ache laced with
nostalgia for the
future

how can you force me
to crave a feeling
you created?

create your universe

you could swim to the
deepest part of my mind
and find that all there is to
drown in are thoughts of you

create your universe

it was a subtle kind of sadness; one that crept up,
just enough to remind you that you're alone. each
passing stranger, each heavy gust of wind and
each fucking star in the sky would remind you of
someone, long enough to laugh in your face and
say, "you're so lonely, aren't you?" you couldn't even
help it. you'd fall back into old habits. maybe you'd
text your ex, call an old friend, even kiss a stranger...
but nothing would satisfy you. hell, you weren't
even sure if you knew what would satisfy you.
how messed up is that? how long can you wait for
someone to show you what happiness is supposed
to feel like? and how long before you just give up?

create your universe

it is the oceans within you
that seek to drown me

never once remorseful,
as they violently roar

for my attention

create your universe

there used to be resilience in her. when the evening
sky opened and the air felt just right, she would search.
she searched for you in the old, dusty stairwells of her
past and the gleaming, sunlit apartments of her future.
she fought days without sleep, only to find nothing but
former keys to the wrong, aching hearts. she believed
you would be where her heart was: near the trees, deep
in the dark blue water of anticipation, but she found
nothing. without you, she was hopeless. she slowly
faded - disappeared into the crowd as if she was just
another face in the city. the will and strength she once
had flew far away. she did not have enough time.

maybe none of us really do.

create your universe

i have waded through the stillness
surrendered to the midnight skies

so why do i not feel
more alive?

i must go -
the mysteries of the wild
are tugging at my heartstrings
and screaming for escape

create your universe

it was the brisk summer wind that slowed her pace and made her heavy. she longed for serenity, and the ability to feel whole; a feeling that disappeared the same as the dew from the morning grass. even her thoughts, her most certain feelings, had been struck with uncertainty. even his love had fallen away.

she walked toward the vicious sea with purpose and belief that the deep blue water would bring her lightness. clarity. transparency.

with her white dress flowing through the wind, she quickly let down her hair and threw her notebook aside as she quickened her pace to a run. with one sudden swoop the wind picked her up and slowly watched her drift into the water, where she would be light and free of the uncertainty that encompassed her. for each wave would bring her further to sea and further into the horizon where, come night, she would be light in a sea of darkness.

create your universe

i am dangerously cautious
a rain pour, if you let me

to think you could watch me
until you drown

would be a most lovely sight

create your universe

what does it take
to feel as if

you may suffocate in the
hurricane you've created

the storm you've built
with life

create your universe

it was a cold day in mid-june, and the clouds hung low in the sky. the raindrops fell slowly onto the newly washed pavement. the road stretched as far as the eye could see. "i believe this road could lead us to the end of the world," you once told me. i was stupid enough to believe you.

the sparrows were hiding in their nests, afraid of the summer shower. afraid of the cold. they feared they would soon disappear from this world, or dissolve away into nothing. the world had constantly been changing, but no one slowed down to notice it.

"do you remember?" you began, one summer night when the sky was dark blue, "you used to lay out here for hours, just staring at the clouds. i'd drive by and barely receive a passing glance. you were so focused on everything else around you, the sky, the trees, but never me. did you not love me then?"

"it wasn't that i didn't love you," i answered slowly, "i just loved everything else a lot more."

create your universe

i watched as the
air swallowed me;
pulled me into its
lungs and asked
me to wilt

how can the very
thing that gives life,
also take it away?

create your universe

your eyes pierce me -
just one look could kill me
if i let it

i long to drink you in
to feel you fill me

completely

create your universe

you are such a
dangerous vision

the scatter of light
before sunset

a violent, most
frightful storm

create your universe

there is mystery
in the fallen echoes
that linger within you

and your mystery
has become my maze

create your universe

it is with wine stained lips
that you coerce me into
oblivion; never stopping to
see what i see, and feel what
i feel in the depths of you.

create your universe

i escape the darkness
suffocating in a room
where my thoughts
speak louder than sound

heavy breathing
slowly lost in
slivers of constellations
that fill my fragile mind

i am at my breaking point
my final word
my last breath

you

create your universe

i'll let the waves
crash over me
pull me under
fill my lungs

i'll gasp for air
the same way
i used to
around you

the butterflies
are drowning,
the salt is
too strong,

the ocean is
melting into
the horizon

i will emerge
and feel
whole again

create your universe

"you are magic," you said

even the stars had to stare
free falling into feeling
breathless, willingly lost
without a care

i don't know what it is
that makes me long for you,
yearn for you -
but my heartstrings
dance for you

and i know,
we are just lost in oblivion
never coming back to life

but if we are together
i know we will be fine

you reach for my waist
in a way that
makes me quiver

i tremble in anticipation
ready for permission
to be yours

what is it about your touch
that forces me into
a spiraling oblivion
i dare not wish to wake up from

we see love
shaped like constellations
and each flicker of a star
brings us closer to
a universe all our own

and i laugh,
because this cannot be real

you. me. infinity.

let me sever the night
into pieces we can swallow

i see entire galaxies
resting in your eyes

with a soul so haunted
mine never stood a chance

for what am i
compared to you?

a minuscule piece
of a grand puzzle

a spectacle
waiting to unfold

create your universe

there is a haze that consumes me
i am restlessly wandering
in my foggy mind

there is a ghost haunting me
imitating my deepest thoughts
pretending to understand

there are strangers meeting
setting off sparks for the very first time
blind to the fires they are starting

there is you, and there is me
unaware of the limbo we are falling into
serenely lusting over eternity

create your universe

your life fills my lungs
and plants flowers there
as if making a home

i have been taught not to
make a home out of a person,
rather a feeling

                    but i cannot
                  feel anything
                other than you

create your universe

if i am magic
you are a miracle

&

this longing between us
is more than a spark -

it is an electric current
destined to destroy

and revive our essence

create your universe

i am naively curious,
unmistakably yours

i could spend forever
trying to write how i feel

watching the sun rise
through your bathroom window
has never felt more beautiful
than it does today

the dim glow of the crisp
fall air, your warmth in
the bed we have started
to share

the wholeness i feel
a complete, thorough feeling
cannot be explained
or matched

and i hope it never is.

create your universe

there is chaos
within my body

an unpredictable force
threatening to unleash
at any moment

there is solitude
within your body

tranquil and quiet
like the walls
of your heart

and as you calm me
i keep you wild

still, when i think about an unbreakable
passion and longing for the unknown, a
desire to fall into the ambiguity of life, i
think about your eyes and how badly i
want to swim in them. live in them. i watch
your pupils open and close as if trying to
tell me stories. i want to make you feel the
way i feel when i read love stories. become
absorbed in the undeniable fearfulness
that is infatuation. you've brought care and
thoughtfulness into my life in a way i never
dreamed possible. and above all, with you,
i feel alive.

i am a wordsmith

i string letters
into something
indescribably yours

but when i think of

the potential
the possibility
the chance

of this being something
i have no words

we could go
somewhere
quiet.

we could find
each other.

we could feel
nothing and
everything.

we could love.
oh, we could
love.

i yearn for your comfort
the way the sea repeatedly
kisses the shore

and want to have you experience
the distress of constantly
craving something more

you make me feel colors
and see sounds unknown to
anyone other than us

floating freely into madness
an infinite night sky
a world built on trust

your very being is a mystery
a complex assortment of treasury
i long to fully understand

you turn to me
and with caring eyes
you call me yours.

"me?"
"you."

create your universe

gravity

"gravity is the natural
attraction between
physical bodies."

create your universe

you are outrageous - this feeling in me strikes like waves during a frightful storm. i lose sight of myself as i am forcefully pulled under. my breathing becomes nonexistent and i sense my time is at its end. i feel apprehension in our distance. there is a longing for closeness in your every word. "i'll be home soon," i whisper, just low enough to keep it to myself. there is no combination of twenty six or twenty eight letters that can describe our intimacy, and the craving i feel for your presence. fearfully, i search for the feeling you've lent me; allowed me to feel in the deepest manner. while the future terrifies me, and i recognize anxiety in its purest form, you calm me. the waves still. the stars show their face. i know i am not alone.

create your universe

i tried to stop it
slow down
fall gently

but the whole point
of love
is how it happens

freely

create your universe

our collision
was explosive

it set fire
to our insides

and left ash
to fill our lungs

and now,

in the midst of
the aftermath

we fearfully find air
in each other

create your universe

wine stained lips
intoxicated on
possibility

dreaming of our
very own forever

fearfully -

for this composition
could be magic

whispered i love yous
tangled in clouds

rain falling
like waterfalls

and us -
finally together, now

come closer
let me show you
what love can be

dive into
the unexpected
hold your breath -

breathe

create your universe

i watched you
plant flowers
in my soul

i watched you
water them
with kindness

and when i tried
to drown them

you were
the sunlight
that kept me alive

create your universe

we are one in the same;
for i am more of me
when you are more of you

create your universe

it was morning,
the city was restless
and we were still

it was daylight, we
kissed, quietly afraid
of the days ahead

it was tuesday,
"i love you,"
i love you, too

create your universe

we are forcefully pulled by gravity
never aware of our bond, but always
close in spirit

create your universe

i have found
such tenderness
in you -

buried in the
shallow waters
of weakness

and the great
depths of love

create your universe

tuck me away

in the safest place of your mind
and let me live in the wonder
that fills your imagination

i want to drown in the ocean
that rages inside of you

and swim along your veins
until your blood stops,
then starts

you consume me
revive me
make me feel whole

let me do the same

create your universe

it is at dusk -

when the sky fills with haze
and slowly fades to black
that i remember

the darkness you lifted me from
and the dawn we built
together

create your universe

kosket minua,
ja putoan sinun
valtamereen

ikuisesti

create your universe

i find myself, slowly -
swimming into unconsciousness
surrounded by champagne filled stars
and a hand-drawn sliver of a moon

i see words, hiding -
on the tip of your tongue
but i cannot kiss you
long enough to taste them

i watch you, carefully -
with eyes full of uncertainty
and wish for you to stay

create your universe

does this intoxication ever vanish?

or will i be drunk
off the thought of you
for the labyrinth of eternity?

you have ruined me
i am scattered among
galaxies not yet found

let me stay this way forever -
impassioned by reflexes unknown
and optimistically yours

create your universe

if this lifelessness consumes me,
drags me to pockets of the universe
know that i will spend my last breath
whispering your name

if nightfall eclipses me,
carries me to the somber part of my mind
know that i will spend my last thought
remembering your eyes

for in darkness we find serenity
in optimism we escape pain
and in you, i've found me
never the same

create your universe

maybe this life is something
we can control and plan

maybe the 382 lives
we have lived before this moment
have taught us how to will
what we need into our lives

but maybe -
this is pure serendipity

or fate in its finest hour
leading me to you

create your universe

the first time i awoke with you was
the very moment i knew sunlight
could exist in people and touch
could be stronger than coffee

create your universe

it is inside your soul
that i can dwell safely

never losing sight
of our completeness

never losing me,
within you

create your universe

there are vacancies that hide
in the depths of your eyes
as they long for someone
to be let inside

i could fill you -

tear down the
blood stained walls
you have built
with your bare hands

and live -

until our house
becomes a home
and our love
becomes our life

create your universe

i used to think of falling in love as some sort
of whirlwind of emotions. the feeling of being
infinite and powerful, yet gracefully free.

i have since learned that love is a combustion
of colors and sounds. a strenuous path to a
universe unknown to anyone else.

the purest, most lovely mystery.

create your universe

it is in our stillness
that i have found you

and in our silence
that i have found me

create your universe

they say home is not a place
but a feeling

i did not know this until
i met you, and now

the very thought of you
is home

create your universe

watching you dream
is like watching poetry unfold

astonishing,
yet calming all at once

create your universe

it is the absence of your
majesty that hollows me

with an overwhelming
longing to be near

and it is your voice
so loud, yet distant

that all the while
keeps me warm

create your universe

there is nothing
so silencing
as the waves
of the sea

pulling all of you
closer to all of me

create your universe

i could not make sense of you
strong hearted and tough
yet fragile at the core
you.

you could not make sense of me
mysteriously cautious
yet certain all the same
me.

they could not make sense of us
mystery at its finest
a vastness disguised in the unknown
us.

create your universe

there was a fire in me
longing to spread
like wildfires in the
deepest woods

there was a downpour in you
more vigorous than all others
eager to drown
even the calmest seas

and together,
we were the perfect storm

create your universe

i cannot comprehend
that time is relative in space
and that one year here,
is seconds somewhere else

but what i know
for my time here on earth

is that i could spend
an eternity alone
for mere hours
with you in infinity

create your universe

i want your hand
on the small of my back
pulling me calmly
into your air

and i want your lips
lightly on mine
reminding me how
it feels to be breathless

create your universe

there is an intimacy
looming in our souls

i have watched each
star align in the sky
to bring me to you

i've read many tales about love and the fear we
have toward intimacy. the ambiguity kills us,
tries to pull us into an ocean so deep we cannot
help but drown. but love is unique in that it
makes you feel okay.

drown me. pull me under. as long as i get to
spend my last breath with you.

with the irresistible
nectar of love
you have taken
me

with the solace
in your being
you have made me
free

create your universe

i let you carve out my insides
you left nothing but bones

a frightful reminder
of what i used to be

how could i fall in love
with such a thief?

create your universe

i fear i am delirious
loving you;

for i have not seen
stars like yours

in our universe

and the cynic in me
does not know if

you are real

create your universe

what does it mean
to love and be loved

with such a fire
that the very touch
would turn you to ash?

create your universe

i return to you in waves of

elation
pain
comfort

no matter the feeling
you are always mine

create your universe

it is in the quiet comfort of your words
that i have built my home

and it is there that i have found
your soul within my own

create your universe

our spiritual affinity is a knot so strong
no threat of storm could ever untie it

create your universe

it wasn't the universe conspiring against me,
or endless gusts of wind pushing me to that
moment. it wasn't the iridescent dark gray sky
or the gleaming lights far in the distance. it
wasn't how i felt in that moment, or how i was
being drawn to your aura. it wasn't just that.

it was the soft graze of your hand on the small
of my back, and the way your mouth puckered
when i tried to make you laugh. it was how you
spun me around and pulled me closer to you
while never losing sight of my eyes. it was your
soft whisper in my ear before parting ways.

maybe night and day could mingle, letting one
breathe while the other gasps for air.

create your universe

you have the unimaginable ability
to make me feel like me again

create your universe

it is as if
the entire light spectrum
falls softly in your eyes

for when i look at you
i see worlds unknown
and sights unseen

everlasting serenity

create your universe

we are of the same stars
the same wandering spirits

loving you is effortless

create your universe

i'm not sure i could ever love you
as deeply as i intend to

but i promise
i'll spend every waking moment

trying

create your universe

the separation of our souls -

my scarlet illusion
your viridian aura

had created an amethyst sky
more haunting than ever

and it was in our absence
i discovered

an imperishable love

create your universe

you have taken my mask
and thrown it to sea

with your kindness
i am finally me

create your universe

i have watched tenderness drip
from your fingertips as you pull me
out of my void and into your world

create your universe

take me back to that world

where the ocean
blurred into the horizon

the waves kissed the rocks
with tenderness

and we fell into
the depths of each other

create your universe

we watched the blue sky
drip with mystery as we
swore that moments like
this could not last forever

we whispered "i love you"
and became tangled in eternity

create your universe

you are there,
forcefully in my
veins, poisoning
my thoughts with
love and my fears
with hope

create your universe

i know i have loved you
some other life
some other time

but that cannot mean
that in this moment
i love you any less

in fact,
it is in this eternity
that i love you the most

create your universe

if there were words to explain
how you make my heartstrings dance
and fill my eyes with waters
of the deepest oceans

i would sing at the top of my lungs
so the world could experience your wonder

i'm terrified of the longing
i know is coming
i curiously question your admiration
and pine for the feeling of being whole

you are unexplainable -
full of the brightest blues
and most sincere stars

there is such thing as magic
and i have found it in your eyes

your thought
your understanding
you

create your universe

you touch me
my head spins into an oblivion
i cannot escape from

your serenity is overwhelming -
the world will never know
this peacefulness

i see you in darkness
i hear you in the quiver of
the warm california breeze

and most of all,
i sense your closeness
in every bone of my being

if our bodies could make art
we would be music, floating
through the arms of the wind

how you turn my anxious cells
into loving laughs,
i'll never know

for i am red

and your touch of blue
turns me into the most
passionate shade of lavender

this world will ever know

create your universe

constellations

"there's chaos to the universe. but there's also drawn lines of the constellations for us to make some sense."

create your universe

the air was still - the earth, motionless. the
stars formed a beautiful constellation above
the figures of you and me. we lay quietly in
the darkness; afraid of disturbing the peace
which rested above our bodies. a serene
breeze caressed our faces, and i moved my
body closer to yours. you took my hand
and brought it near your face.

the earth stood still with you by my side.
there was no place i would have rather
been. you were my thoughts, my cries,
my melodies. it was always you.

create your universe

don't you know,

there are stars in skies
we will never see

feelings to be felt
with grave uncertainty

but i find comfort in knowing

everything i have yet
to experience

i will get to do with you

create your universe

our souls have lived
many lifetimes
fondly side by side,
of that i am sure

it is like an experiment -
experiencing you
for the first time
again

trying to find familiarity
in what may have once been

our love is frivolous -
as eternal as
we allow it to be

saving each other,
to save ourselves

you and i are from
the same dust
the same star
the same galaxy

and in finding you,
i've discovered me

create your universe

you and i are of
esoteric nature

born from vicious tides
and lost mosaics

never fully
understood

create your universe

i saw bright life
in the glass eyes
of your soul

i heard pain drip
from the caring
touch of your hands

i felt love in your
whispers, as they
fell around me

create your universe

our love is a language
i am patiently learning
and our souls tell a story
i will spend my lifetime
trying to write

c

create your universe

we bathed in lust
and fearlessness

i watched the universe
twirl around our
private utopia

and all the while,
you never lost sight
of my eyes

create your universe

you,
with your wonderment
and benevolence
steal what's left
of my creation

my essence is of you
yesterday at 12:53am
tomorrow at 7:34am

now.

create your universe

if you find me
lost along the way

bring me to lavender skies
turquoise ambiance
and the deepest red vessels

of home

create your universe

it was in that moment -

the change of the year
the calm after the chaos

that she had finally grasped
the unseen light

a renewal all her own

create your universe

she will tie your words
into bouquets of clever
sentences. she will plant
flowers in the crevices
of your mind;

and when you fall in love
with a writer, your flowers
never die

create your universe

there is no sense in
loving without passion
living without freedom
breathing to survive

inhale strength
exhale greatness
and find your clarity
in the haziness of life

create your universe

what if we have not fully lived our experiences until after the initial instance? what if our happiness, our sadness, and our angst can only be felt once the moment has passed? we never, in the moment, experience the most sincere feelings; but rather fragments of the whole emotion. it is not until we relive the past that these feelings can be felt in their entirety.

create your universe

i have fallen into the unexplored

light of an early morning
mysterious depths of the ocean

and in this stillness -
these looming depths

i will find myself

create your universe

if you let yourself
float in the wind

get lost in your
own potential

you will see
that you are

       limitless

the real secret of life
is to find happiness
within yourself

and give it away to others

create your universe

you can be swallowed
by darkness, or rise
to meet the sunlit skies
of your future;

the beauty is that the
choice is always yours

create your universe

do not take caution when
the seas roar with anger.
the waters you drift in
will always lead you home.

create your universe

find a sanctuary to get lost in

where art flows like blood
from your fingertips

and new life is born

create your universe

stop worrying and aching
about what life is
supposed to look like

create your own rules
so you can break them
and be free

create your universe

our souls are full of fire
built from the words
of those who fan our flames

create your universe

you will have to break
before you heal

succumb to pressure
before you can renew again

then you will find yourself

alive
awake
inspired

reborn

create your universe

i found myself lost in another universe. one much larger and more cynical than this. where the skies would open with red gusts of wind and gray drops of rain. where mountains were built from water and the seas froze over.

i had searched for myself here, where they had told me i would be happier. "just try something new," they said, not realizing that they were asking me to conform. and i was not them. my happiness was not theirs to decide. and in those frightening moments, i found my light. my hope. my passion. and at last, i was myself.

create your universe

it is not life if you are not
challenged and changed
in each passing moment.
stagnancy is a forceful
death wish.

create your universe

through each happy
and sorrowful day

i will always be in love
with the storm of our lives

c

love is a delicacy -
a sun ray that illuminates
the luckiest

and leaves serenity
in a world of tired eyes

create your universe

there are wild words
hidden in the small
crevices of your mind

find them,
release them,
watch them dance

for they are
a masterpiece
waiting to unfold

create your universe

let the happiness you seek
be something you find

when you pour yourself
into what you love

and still feel whole

create your universe

do not disguise your

faults
flaws
or imperfections -

wear them proudly
and let the world know
how hard you fought

to become yourself

do not take the adventures
of your life lightly. fall
in love with what makes
you feel. exhale the air
that suffocates you. and
remember, you are free.

create your universe

life is merely a domino
effect of our decisions
and consequences. this
does not rule your life.

you decide when
to restart your pieces.

create your universe

our fears are illuminated
by the light of the midnight
sun, and swallowed by the
silence of the fatal night

create your universe

what are words if they do not graze the sky
with love as they fall from caring mouths? if
they do not seep into your veins until each
syllable pulses within you?

words are created to be expressed. they are
spoken to be loved. they are written to be felt.

create your universe

if it is contentment you seek
you must first bury yourself
in the abyss of your soul;

to be alone within your body
is to love every fragment,
every thought, every silence

until you are ready to love
another

create your universe

i found myself lost in curiosity
skimming the surface of all
there is to explore

until i dove under
and found the pieces of life
that were buried in me

create your universe

be still -

surrender to that which
makes your soul ache

remember your passions

and tear down the walls
that try to contain you

your life is a miracle
and your light is your own

create your universe

live with an abundance
of delicacies. be gentle,
first with yourself, then
with others.

do not forget your tenderness,
even on the most callous days

create your universe

to be understood in silence
is to be one with each breath
that echoes from the walls
of your soul. to be one with
your thoughts, deeply rooted
in the caves of your heart.

to be understood in silence
is to be loved

create your universe

life is a careful blend of reactions and uncertainty. the mindless juxtaposition of sorrow and excitement. the endless road to an unforeseeable future.

i hope that is always enough for you.

create your universe

there are people in life
more precious than any
gems, more lively than
any ocean, and more
inspirational than any
story. hold on to them

create your universe

there is life, fearfully hiding
beyond the "what if's"
we are waiting for.

but this is life.
this is it.

create your universe

as i end this journey, i stop
to wonder about you and
the complexity of us. the
fearlessness we stumbled into.
the strength we found in each
other. the love; oh, the love.

create your universe

it was the calm air of july that
swallowed me. i was restless
in its embrace, digging graves
for my feelings and planting
flowers of courage in each ray
of sunlight.

you were not my own, the way
i am my own. but i am more
of you than me and our souls
have tangled far too deeply to
be undone. not in this lifetime.
not on this earth.

not in my universe.

create your universe

you have been a beautiful fight
a love worth dying for
a mysterious entity

and without a doubt

today,
tomorrow
infinitely

you are mine.

i am my own -

for i was born from the stars
that surround me, and fought
through the dark matter that
longed to consume me.

this is only the beginning.

there is a universe
of secrets inside of me.

c

acknowledgements;

thank you for joining me on this journey

extra thanks to:

my family, for their unconditional love and
support of everything i have ever done

cody, for stirring these feelings inside of me
(and encouraging me to write about them)

my closest friends, for always believing in
my wildest dreams

emily, for your thoughtful edits and kind
words of wisdom

and you, for reading each word and
creating your own universe

i hope you have built your own universe,
and fallen deeply in love with all it contains

Made in the USA
San Bernardino, CA
06 November 2015